WAIKIKI
YESTERYEAR

By Glen Grant

MUTUAL PUBLISHING

In this 1850 Burgess lithograph of Waikiki, depicting community life, we see the work ethic of this society. While the men in the foreground prepare their fishing canoes and nets, others return from a day on the water. Women collect *limu* (seaweed) near the shore and tend to *na keiki* (children). The Hawaiian culture was one of communal sharing, each member within the extended village family working to contribute to the prosperity of the whole. *Baker-Van Dyke Collection*

An Ancient Tradition

Waikiki Before 1900

For people around the world, Waikiki evokes images both alluring and magical. Even in ancient times, the beach, the warm, predictable sun, the cooling breezes, the rolling surf, the exquisitely tinted sunsets, and the full moon inspired romance and legend. The aura of Waikiki is not a modern creation of public relations, but is ingrained in this place filled with beauty and history.

Waikiki, meaning "spouting waters" in Hawaiian, was hundreds of years ago a

Women, especially of *ali'i* (chiefly) families, enjoyed the ancient sport of surfing as much as the men. 1860. *Baker-Van Dyke Collection.*

major seat of government and cultural activity on O'ahu. The *ali'i* or chiefs chose its placid shores, extensive ponds, and streams for their estates more than 500 years ago, well before the first arrival of western foreigners in 1792. They planted thousands of coconut trees on the shore and built *lo'i* or taro fields over the low-lying wetlands behind the beach.

An extensive system of fishponds was developed in Waikiki, created in the many *muliwai* or brackish waters where several rivers met the ocean. Thousands of *maka'ainana* or people lived in the large *ahupua'a* or land division of Waikiki. Farmers in the valley shared their crops of taro, sweet potato, or banana with fishermen who caught fish from the bay's fertile

waters or gathered shellfish along the shore. In the worship of their ancient *akua* or gods, at least seven *heiau* or temples were built in Waikiki, including Helumoa at the site of the current-day Royal Hawaiian Hotel and Papa'ena'ena on the slopes of Diamond Head, then known as Le'ahi.

Kakuhihewa was among the greatest ancient chiefs to have resided at Waikiki, having lived during the 16th century at Ulukou, a royal compound located today on the grounds of the Moana Surfrider Hotel. Celebrated in legend and song, Kakuhihewa brought to Waikiki a golden age of prosperity and cultural enrichment under a reign characterized by powerful leadership. He was said to have planted the first coconuts which would eventually grow into the Helumoa grove of 10,000 trees on the grounds of the current Royal Hawaiian Hotel.

Waikiki's recorded history begins in 1795, when the armies of Kamehameha from the island of Hawai'i landed at Waikiki and at Waiala'e on the other side of Diamond Head. Triumphant in his control of the islands of Hawai'i, Maui, Lana'i, Kaho'olawe, and Moloka'i, Kamehameha threw his full force against the defending armies of Kalanikupule on the island of O'ahu. The fighting on Waikiki beach was fierce as the defenders retreated to Nu'uanu Valley where they were finally vanquished. In deference to Waikiki's tradition as O'ahu's seat of power, Kamehameha erected a coral-stone house and *heiau*, preparing for his final conquest—the island of Kaua'i.

In anticipation of the invasion of Kaua'i, Kamehameha built up a powerful invasion army on the beach at Waikiki in 1804. Before this great force was ready to launch their canoes across the channel, a terrible disease swept through them, crippling their ability to carry out the conquest of Kaua'i. It wasn't until 1810, after peaceful negotiations with the chief of Kaua'i, that Kamehameha would finally be able to claim himself *mo'i* or "king" of the Hawaiian Islands.

As Kamehameha politically united the islands under one central government, other changes rapidly came to Waikiki. *Haole* or foreigners had arrived with their big ships, which carried to Hawai'i iron, guns, cannons, cloth, and diseases.

Although Waikiki was a picturesque beach, it was not a safe anchorage for the deep-draft hulls of the foreign ships. Instead, the newcomers found a break in the coral reef and a safe anchorage about three miles away, near the village called Kou. This harbor provided excellent protection, a good source of freshwater from Nu'uanu Stream, and suitable food supplies in the nearby village. The foreigners began to call this

Dressed in a maritime vest, European-style hat, and traditional *malo* (loincloth), this man carries his calabash cargo across town to Waikiki. 1852. *Baker-Van Dyke Collection*

anchorage Honolulu or "Fair Haven," as *haole* merchants, sandalwood traders, whalers, and explorers began to settle in the once quiet village. As the harbor became an active center for foreign traffic and trade, Kamehameha moved his compound on O'ahu to the shores of Honolulu, where a subsequent capital was established.

The political abandonment of Waikiki marked a decisive turn in Hawaiian affairs. Less and less were wealth and power based on fertile fields and rich fisheries; chiefs with real power had foreign ships, guns, cloth, and the artifacts of foreign nations. The arrival of American Protestant missionaries, the introduction of a foreign god, and *palapala* or writing further accelerated deep-seated cultural changes. The highly intricate Hawaiian way of life was being abandoned as manufactured goods, the concept of private property, salaried employment, and the lure of foreign things flooded into the Islands.

Foreign diseases also had a devastating impact upon Waikiki, which had once been a densely populated area on O'ahu. The 1804 epidemic which devastated Kamehameha's army at Waikiki was called *ma'i oku'u* by Hawaiians—modern authorities suggest that it may have been cholera or possibly typhoid fever. A smallpox-infested sailor on a quarantined ship swam to shore at Waikiki in 1853 seeking the comfort of female companionship. As a result, smallpox raged through the district and Honolulu, infecting and killing over 3,000 Hawaiians. The rising death rates correlated with a plummeting birth rate as venereal diseases left the native wombs barren.

By 1866 Mark Twain noted that Waikiki was an "historic area" with the remnants of an ancient village. Visitors would ask the residents what had happened to the thousands of Hawaiians who had once occupied these beautiful shores. The answer given was a simple, tragic, *kanaka pau*—"the people are gone." Foreign diseases and epidemics eventually reduced the total Hawaiian population throughout the Islands from an estimated 300,000–800,000 people in 1790 to 40,000 in 1890. The lonely beach of Waikiki was stark evidence of this tragic chapter in Hawai'i's past.

As Waikiki came to be "remote" and "countryside" by the end of the nineteenth century, its emptied beaches and languishing shade trees became an excellent retreat for town-worn visitors. Far from the watchful eye of the missionary-based Protestant churches, Waikiki was also a place to revive ancient cultural practices, dance, and song which had gone "underground" with the introduction of "blue-nose" morality. The royal families and well-to-do merchants built summer retreats on the former sacred compounds of Helumoa and Ulukou, the current locations of the Royal Hawaiian and Moana Surfrider Hotels. Building modest cottages set amid broad lawns, old coconut groves, and meandering streams, royalty and

their often distinguished guests held all-day *lu'au* or feast and surfed, swam, fished, drank, took naps, or simply did nothing at all—activities that still count among Waikiki's noblest traditions.

King David Kalakaua, who reigned from 1874 to 1891, threw huge *lu'au* for visiting dignitaries at Waikiki. The "Merrie Monarch" thought so much of Waikiki's restorative powers that he donated 200 acres of it for a park. Named for his queen,

Selected by Queen Lili'uokalani to be her successor to the Hawaiian throne, Princess Ka'iulani was destined for a tragic turn of events. On January 17, 1893, the Hawaiian monarchy was overthrown by a group of Honolulu businessmen backed by American military forces. Five years later, despite pleas for justice by Queen Lili'uokalani to restore the independence of the Hawaiian kingdom, the Islands were annexed by the United States.

A foreigner's interpretation of surfing at Waikiki. Boards of 5 to 15 feet long were molded into elongated "tombstone" shapes and stained with the pounded bark of kukui nut trees. This fanciful painting was rendered by someone who never caught a wave. Surfers ride along the face of a rising swell, not straight down on its breaking curl. Nevertheless, there is still the feel of the surfers' excitement as they ride the waves in an idyllic setting. Watercolor, circa 1860. *Baker-Van Dyke Collection*

Kapi'olani, it opened with an enormous celebration on Kamehameha Day, 1877.

The King's niece and heiress to the throne, the sublimely beautiful Princess Ka'iulani, lived near Kapi'olani Park and rode her pony, Fairy, along its bridal paths and across its quaint footbridges. Quick-witted and charming, Ka'iulani captivated all who knew her. It was a great loss to Waikiki when the young princess went away to England for schooling. During her life overseas, Ka'iulani acquired the elegant grace of a genteel era while attracting the attention of more than one royal suitor.

Princess Ka'iulani returned to her fine house at 'Ainahau in Waikiki. There, among loyal advisors and tame peacocks, the now-reclusive princess spent the last years of her short life mourning the dispossession of the Hawaiian people and the loss of the monarchy. At the young age of 24, she died at her Waikiki home in the early hours of March 6, 1899. Those who were at her side said that at the moment she died, her beloved peacocks began a shrill, piercing cry. Waikiki's royal era had come to an end.

As the 20th century dawned, Waikiki witnessed a new resident on its beaches—

a variety of opulent mansions that characterized the reign of King Sugar. Wealthy sugar "barons," financiers, and shipping magnates built distinctive homes on the shore along Kapi'olani Park and on the slopes of Diamond Head. More and more bathhouses were erected on the beach to receive Honolulu denizens seeking the restorative effects of "surf bathing." A visitor noted that Waikiki's "seaside felicity" gave the "promise of rest in its motionless life, and a chance for self- recovery in its self-forgetful solitude."

Visitors from around the world slowly began to also discover the charms of Waikiki. By the mid-1880's, tourist travel to Hawai'i was still in its infancy—a round-trip passage to Honolulu from San Francisco aboard Oceanic Lines' *Mariposa*, *Alameda*, *Zealandia*, or *Australia* (seven days each way) was an expensive $125. In 1886, Hawai'i welcomed 2,040 visitors. If they stayed on O'ahu, the hotels and other accommodations were mostly in downtown Honolulu.

Visitors to Waikiki first rode on mule-drawn trolleys (later replaced by electric streetcars) which began trundling day-trippers the three dusty miles from Honolulu to Waikiki via Waikiki Road (now Kalakaua Avenue) in 1889. The bathhouses offered a towel, a swimsuit, dressing rooms, and a sandy stretch of beach—for a fee. One, the ornate Waikiki Villa (located on the site of the Sheraton Waikiki), even offered overnight sleeping rooms and introduced Saturday night dancing to Honolulu. A saloon owner opened the Long Branch Baths at Ulukou and put up a 200-foot-long "marine toboggan" to lure business.

The popularity of the Waikiki bathhouses did not go unnoticed by Honolulu's hoteliers and businessmen. The luxurious downtown Hawaiian Hotel bought the Waikiki Villa bathhouse and operated it as a beach annex for guests. At the other end of Waikiki, the 10-room Park Beach Hotel opened in 1888, becoming one of the first hotels in Waikiki. Business, however, was very poor and the hotel closed less than a year later. Waikiki was still too far and remote to attract visitors for an overnight stay.

The 20-room Sans Souci opened in 1893 as Waikiki's first successful hotel. Noted for its famous visitors, tropical gardens, and castaway ambiance, the establishment reverted to a private residence before the turn of the century. San Souci, "without care," survives as the name of the curved high-rise condominium on the site.

Waikiki at the beginning of the twentieth century was a curious blend of ancient and modern, as a Polynesian lifestyle slowly faded under the growing hustle-and-bustle of a rising tide of tourism. Visitors in straw boaters and three-piece suits shared the sand with fishermen (in simple *malo* or loin cloths), who tended nets and stored their canoes in the *hau* thickets and *naupaka* beds at the upper edges of the beach, as their ancestors had done hundreds of years earlier. Chinese farmers had moved into Waikiki to grow rice and raise ducks in the old taro ponds behind the beach, near the clanging trolley cars which carried noisy revelers to the popular bathhouses. The beach was still dominated by its thousands of old palms, although the broad, open lawns beneath the towering trees were being crowded by forests of thorny *kiawe* or mesquite, introduced from Australia, and banyans brought from India. The balmy air and gentle waters were unchanged, although among the unwelcome new arrivals was the bothersome mosquito who loved Waikiki's fishponds and rice farms.

Scant physical evidence of the early Hawaiian era is found in today's Waikiki. The ancient streams which fed to fishponds and *lo'i* have all been diverted into the Ala Wai Canal. The lowlands, where farmer and fisherman helped weave a civilization of sharing and aloha, have been drained and covered with a dense layer of urbanity that towers over Diamond Head. The stone edifices of the great temples where the people of old worshipped their powerful dieties have all vanished, their *mana* or divine power preserved only in the ancient stories and myths, and in song, dance, and tale.

The search for ancient Waikiki reveals a hidden cluster of sacred stones, a few place names on street signs, and a grove of old coconut trees, the descendants of the famous sacred grove at Helumoa linked through legend to the great chief Kakuhihewa. The modern-day visitor or island resident who takes the time to search these few treasures out can for a brief moment journey back to old Waikiki. Through the portraits captured on film and the stories passed on through the generations, Waikiki's yesteryears can once again come to life.

Lahainaluna Engraving of "Diamond Hill" from Honolulu. The landmark got its name from early British sailors who mistakenly believed the olivine crystals in the lava rocks on its slopes were diamonds. The stone wall in the foreground suggests the outer boundaries of a *heiau*. Ancient Waikiki, with its balmy, leeward weather and dramatic beauty, has long been a protected place of peace and wealth. *Baker-Van Dyke Collection*

The smallpox epidemic in Hawai'i began in May 1853 and ended in January 1854, claiming 6,000 lives. The swift outbreak made it impossible to vaccinate the general public, resulting in the tragic reduction of a very vulnerable native population. This tiny grass shack in Waikiki served as the only hospital treating the victims of the smallpox virus. The exact location of this humble house of healing is not known. Many believed Waikiki to be a healing place, an area with regenerative powers. *Drawing by Paul Emmert. The Hawaiian Historical Society*

The port of Honolulu, sketched during the month when Melville enlisted on the frigate *United States*. To the left of Diamond Head is its sister crater, Puowaina (Punchbowl), located three miles east and directly *mauka* (toward the mountains) of Honolulu Harbor. The coconut groves of Waikiki were so prominent, they are used in this rendering to identify the region. In the 1800s, Waikiki was considered a rural area in comparison to the rapidly growing conglomeration of buildings around Honolulu Harbor. *Baker-Van Dyke Collection*

One of Lot Kamehameha's (King Kamehameha V) grass huts at his Waikiki retreat. The tall palms seen here (and in the following illustrations) were part of the famous ancient grove of Helumoa, planted by the great O'ahu chief Kakuhihewa in the late 1500s. *Baker-Van Dyke Collection*

The view of Le'ahi (Diamond Head) along the beach fronting King Kamehameha V's beach house in 1865. Today it is the site of the Royal Hawaiian Hotel, which preserves in its east courtyard the last remnant of the Helumoa grove, once numbering 10,000 palms. *Baker-Van Dyke Collection*

An artist's rendering of a *pa'u*-clad woman riding through the coconut grove at Kamehameha V's Waikiki residence. The word *pa'u* is a general term for a "skirt" of any kind. This type of *pa'u* was the traditional dress for women on horseback in the 1850s. Horses belonged to the *ali'i* (ruling class), and in keeping with fashion, noble women wore long, flowing skirts and short, shoulder cloaks. *Baker-Van Dyke Collection*

The Royal Helumoa grove of niu (coconut trees), planted by Kakuhihewa, the greatest O'ahu ali'i, is depicted in this watercolor by Helen Whitney Kelley. Ponds, fed by springs and mountain streams of Manoa and Palolo valleys, dotted the Waikiki landscape. In later years, as foreigners moved into the area, lilies and reed were added as a decorative touch. *Bishop Museum Archives.*

King Lot, Kamehameha V's home at Waikiki as it looked in 1870. The water in the foreground is the 'Apuakehau Stream, fed by waters that drained from the mountain valleys of Manoa, Makiki, and Palolo. The ancient coconut grove laced through the entire royal acreage in the Waikiki area. After Lot's death in 1872, his beachfront *kauhale* (housing compound) continued to serve as a retreat for Hawai'i's royalty. *Hawai'i State Archives*

A photo taken by Henry Chase in the 1860s of a "modern" dwelling built on Kamehameha V's Waikiki property. Lot was the last of the Kamehameha kings. His successor, Prince William Lunalilo, became king by special election of the Legislative Assembly.
Baker-Van Dyke Collection

View of Diamond Head and the Waikiki shoreline, with Robert Louis Stevenson's retreat barely seen in the center-right. 1890. *Baker-Van Dyke Collection*

The end of the mule-drawn tramcar line, located at the expansive bridge where the present Kapahulu Avenue meets Kalakaua Avenue, late 1880s. The sign above reads, "Driving faster than a walk over the bridge will be prosecuted according to the law." *Baker-Van Dyke Collection*

Waikiki (the name means "spouting waters") supported widespread wetland agriculture. Banana, rice, and taro fields border Waikiki Road (presently Kalakaua Avenue) near its intersection with McCully Street. Notice the rails for the tram line. 1898. *Baker-Van Dyke Collection*

SACRED POHAKU

In the colorful mayhem of modern Waikiki, as sun-tanned visitors pack the beaches or browse through the myriad souvenir shops, four ancient *pohaku* or stones rest on Kuhio Beach, silent reminders of Hawai'i's rich past. With the sweeping changes that have occurred in modern Hawai'i since World War II, transforming Waikiki into a major urban resort destination, it is fortunate that these sacred remnants of a 2,000-year-old civilization have survived. They invite the curious to journey to forgotten Waikiki and recall the history of *ka po'e kahiko*, "the people of old." In the shadow of majestic Le'ahi or "Diamond Head," they have witnessed generations of chiefs, commoners, and foreigners forge O'ahu's history.

One of Princess Ka'iulani's pet peacocks perches atop a "wizard stone" on the grounds of 'Ainahau. The stone will later be moved to Kuhio beach. Circa 1898. *Baker-Van Dyke Collection*

The four *pohaku* were originally placed in a sacred compound by four *kahuna* or priests around the year 1400 A.D. This area, where the Moana Surfrider Hotel now stands, was known as Ulukou or "grove of the kou tree."

According to a legend recorded by Queen Lili'uokalani, these four priests, named Kapaemahu, Kahaloa, Kapuni, and Kinohi, came to the Hawaiian Islands from Tahiti and lived at Ulukou for many years, teaching medicinal and healing arts to the people of O'ahu.

Deciding to return to Tahiti, the priests directed the people to bring to Ulukou four large stones found in Kaimuki. On the night of Po Kane—the legendary appearance of the night marcher spirits—thousands of kama'aina helped move the stones to their location in Waikiki. As the sun crested the Ko'olau mountains, ceremonies were performed and *ki'i* or images were placed beneath each rock. Before setting sail for their distant island home, the four priests placed their hands upon the stones and imparted their *mana* or divine power, leaving their essence and knowledge to help those they left behind.

The rocks each had a different purpose. Kapuni, according to Queen Lili'uokalani, was "a peculiar shaped coral boulder from the sea that was noted for the waves breaking over it."

A favorite sport in ancient times was to stand on Kapuni as the waves engulfed the stone. The *pohaku* were positioned opposite a place on the outer reef called the "Cave of the Shark God." Fishermen, swimmers, and surfers used the rocks as guides to avoid the cave.

The *pohaku* remained on the beach for hundreds of years, providing spiritual healing to any who made offerings and prayer. They stood as silent witnesses to the passing of time in Waikiki.

Governor Cleghorn inherited the stones when he bought his Waikiki estate called 'Ainahau in 1907. He had them dug out of the sand and placed in a more prominent position on his property. Princess Likelike, the wife of Governor Archibald Cleghorn and their daughter, Princess Ka'iulani, never entered the waters of Waikiki without placing a flower lei upon the stones and offering a prayer.

When Cleghorn passed away in 1910, his will stated that "it is my wish and I hereby direct that the historical stones now upon the premises...shall not be defaced or removed from said premises."

The sacred stones of Waikiki remained on the beach fronting the Moana Hotel until the 1920s, when they mysteriously disappeared. Forty years later, when the Waikiki Bowling Alley on Kalakaua Avenue was demolished, construction workers found four large boulders supporting the foundation of the building. Long-time Waikiki residents identified the lost sacred stones. The four "wizards" had been improperly dragged into the foundation years earlier to hold up the bowling alley! They were finally relocated in their current place of honor on Kuhio Beach through the efforts of the Waikiki Improvement Association and the City and County of Honolulu.

The next time you are strolling along the sands of Kuhio Beach near the Honolulu Police Department's Waikiki substation on Kalakaua Avenue, take a moment to search out these relics of Hawai'i's past. They are still holding constant vigil in this place of changing *mana*.

Waikiki *keiki* (children) take a break in their play to pose for the photographer, facing inland at the mouth of Ku'ekaunahi Stream. This waterway flowed along what is now Kapahulu Avenue and emptied into the bay at Kuhio Beach where the jettied drainage pipe now stands. 1886. *A. Mitchell, Bishop Museum*

The family of W.W. Hall coming from Kapahulu Avenue near Waiala'e on the backside of Waikiki to their beach residence, now the site of the Halekulani Hotel. The flat, well-irrigated Kapahulu area was once dotted with banana, taro, and rice farms. Today it is a gateway to Waikiki. A powerful businessman, Hall was a key figure in the 1893 Overthrow. *Bishop Museum*

One of the most famous *lu'au* in Hawaiian history, hosted by King Kalakaua, in honor of Robert Louis Stevenson and his mother. Seated next to the King is his sister, the future Queen Lili'uokalani. The event took place at "Manuia Lanai," the Henry Poor residence in Waikiki, February 1889. *Baker-Van Dyke Collection*

$\mathcal{R}$OYAL WAIKIKI

During his 1889 visit to the Hawaiian Islands, Robert Louis Stevenson spent many hours in the company of King David Kalakaua. *Baker-Van Dyke Collection*

Lili'uokalani shares a thoughtful moment with the esteemed author. Stevenson stayed for five weeks at the Sans Souci hotel in Waikiki in 1893, prior to his last voyage home to Samoa. *Hawai'i State Archives*

Waikiki's royal heritage reaches back in time to the great chief Mailikukahi, who first established the beach as a seat of power for the island of Oʻahu about 1450 A.D. Nearly 150 years later, the greatest Oʻahu chief, Kakuhihewa, reigned at Ulukou. So powerful was this 16th-century chief that Waikiki beach was often referred to in chant as *ke oneʻai aliʻi o Kakuhihewa* or the "chief-consuming sands of

King Kamehameha the Great, Hawaiʻi's first modern monarch. By 1810 he had accomplished what no other high chief was capable of—the unification of all the islands under one rule. *Hawaiʻi State Archives*

Kakuhihewa." Invading armies that dared land at Waikiki during the reign of this famous chief died on the beach.

In 1795, Kamehameha, chief of Hawaiʻi and later to be King of the Hawaiian kingdom, landed thousands of men in canoes onto Waikiki's shores in his attempt to acquire the island of Oʻahu. The battle began at present-day Kuhio Beach, then continued to Punchbowl Crater, before his warriors finally defeated Kakuhihewa's army in Nuʻuanu Valley. The remnants of the broken, defending army fled over the mountainous Pali pass to avoid capture, many of them falling to their deaths from the precipitous cliffs. Following his conquest of Oʻahu, Kamehameha and his favorite wife, Kaʻahumanu, are believed to have resided in Waikiki at the sacred grounds of Ulukou.

When Captain George Vancouver visited the Hawaiian Islands in 1792, he became one of the first *haole* or foreigners to see "Whyteete Bay." Describing the village as "numerous, large and in good repair," Captain Vancouver visited Kamehameha's home, constructed of wood and stone.

One of Waikiki's most famous royal residents was King Kalakaua, who lived in a cottage on the grounds called Uluniu, near the current Hyatt Regency Hotel. An avid nationalist who sought to restore the health, culture, and welfare of his native people, Kalakaua revived ancient hula and music, preserved traditional storytelling, and brought the monarchy to its height of pride with the building of the ʻIolani Palace. During His Majesty's reign, Honolulu had become a bustling cosmopolitan Pacific port, as the streets teemed with newly arrived Chinese and Japanese immigrants; trolley cars clanged through the busy thoroughfares; and the construction of new buildings created persistent clatter.

A favorite retreat for His Majesty was his Uluniu estate, often a setting for lavish parties. The Kingdom's most distinguished visitors were entertained in royal fashion at Waikiki. Erudite and quick-witted, the well-read Kalakaua impressed many literati who passed through the Islands, including Robert Louis Stevenson, who enjoyed the King's company during his 1889 visit to Waikiki. Today the only reminder of the Uluniu royal beach house is the street name at Kalakaua Avenue which marks its former location.

Next door to Uluniu was the home of Princess Liliʻuokalani, who became Queen in 1893, following the death of her brother, Kalakaua. Her home was a simple cottage named Hamohamo, located near the current-day intersection of Liliʻuokalani Street and Ala Wai Boulevard. In 1869 one of the largest *luʻau* ever held in Waikiki took place at her home in honor of the first British royal family member to visit Hawaiʻi—the Duke of Edinburgh. This full-day affair was a lavish royal *luʻau* that, according to the missionary press, included performances of the "disgraceful Hula dance." Far from the disapproving eyes of the missionary-dominated moralists of Honolulu, Waikiki was often the scene of games, dances, and sports which were considered "frivolous" or "improper" by Protestant missionaries.

Until her death in 1917, Queen Liliʻuokalani often stayed at Hamohamo in Waikiki for rest, sleep, and bathing. Old-time residents still remember that, as the carriage carrying the Queen passed along Kalakaua Avenue, all the Hawaiians stopped, doffed their hats, and bowed silently until she passed. In the evening the Queen would walk to her boat house, which was on a pier extended into the ocean at Kealohilani Street. The "Queen's pier" became an historic landmark on the beach at Waikiki—well-known as a setting for young lovers to "spoon" on a full-moon night.

Sometimes the Queen would walk out to the "stone wall," where the Ohua Street gang of beachboys was often found strum-

Queen Liliʻuokalani, Hawaiʻi's last monarch. In 1893 a coalition of American businessmen staged an armed but bloodless coup against her government. *Hawaiʻi State Archives*

ming their ukuleles. Tipping them for their musical efforts, she enjoyed the lively *hapa-haole* or "half-white" music which these amateur musicians often created.

One of the residents of Waikiki who also enjoyed the beachboy music along the "stone wall" was the Queen's nephew, Prince Jonah Kuhio Kalanianaʻole, or, as he was affectionately called, "Prince Cupid." The Prince was often seen strolling briskly down Kalakaua Avenue, looking dapper in his three-piece suit, his fedora with a feather lei, his gold-tipped cane and white gloves, and his black, waxed mustache. After the death of Queen Liliʻuokalani in 1917, the Prince inherited beachfront property, where he built a handsome home called Pualeilani on Kalakaua Avenue facing Liliʻuokalani Street. While Kuhio often let the neighborhood children use the beach in front of his property, they were warned not to pick the mangoes from the tree in this yard. As one Waikiki resident remembered many years later, the Prince's wife, Princess Elizabeth Kahanu Kaʻauwai Kalanianaʻole, was known to chase after the children who stole her mangoes!

THE BATTLE OF DIAMOND HEAD

Prince Kuhio was also involved in one of the more interesting historic events in Waikiki—the so-called "Battle of Diamond Head." After the overthrow of Queen Lili'uokalani in 1893 and the subsequent creation of the Republic of Hawai'i in 1894, royalists staged an armed attempt to restore the Queen to her throne. On the evening of January 6, 1895, the royalists transported guns from an off-shore sloop to the home of Henry F. Bertlemann, which was located next-door to the Sans Souci Hotel—close to where the Natatorium is today located. The proprietor of the Sans Souci, Greek entrepreneur George Lycurgus, was another royalist supporter. One of the early hotels in Waikiki, Lycurgus' establishment would become famous when the famed author Robert Louis Stevenson stayed there during his 1893 visit to the Islands.

As Lycurgus, Bertlemann, Prince Kuhio, and over 150 royalists under the leadership of Robert Wilcox and Samuel Nowlein now prepared to overthrow the Republic of Hawai'i, they were interrupted by the sheriff and his posse. Tipped off to the revolt, Republican troops arrived at the Bertlemann house, aborting the rebellion. Shots were exchanged as the royalists fled to Diamond Head, where the battle continued for several days. The remnants of the royalist army then scurried to Palolo Valley, being captured in the upper recesses of Manoa Valley, where they had finally fled in desperation. Participants in the plot, including Prince Kuhio and George Lycurgus, were all sentenced to terms in O'ahu Prison. Queen Lili'uokalani herself was put under house arrest in her own palace for several months in 1895. After he was released from prison, Prince Kuhio later became the Hawai'i delegate to the United States Congress, where he helped to create the Hawaiian Home Lands Act, opening homestead lands for Native Hawaiians. Lycurgus lost his Sans Souci Hotel and eventually became the colorful, well-known proprietor of the Volcano House at Kilauea Crater on the island of Hawai'i.

Where the government posse caught the rebels: Henry Bertlemann's home in Waikiki as it appeared in an illustration in the *San Francisco Examiner*. 1895. *Baker-Van Dyke Collection*

Prince Jonah Kuhio Kalaniana'ole Pi'ikoi, nicknamed "Prince Cupid," would win ten elections as Delegate to Congress and serve from 1903 until his death in 1922. *Bishop Museum*

Passes for historian Dr. N.B. Emerson and friends to visit the Bertlemann home at Waikiki, headquarters for the failed "counterrevolution" staged by royalists in 1895. *Baker-Van Dyke Collection*

Princess Elizabeth Kahanu Ka'auwai Kalaniana'ole, wife of Prince Kuhio, reclines on the circular settee in the parlor of their "Pualeilani" mansion on Waikiki beach. The couple furnished the home with pieces once belonging to their uncle, King David Kalakaua. Circa 1920. *Bishop Museum*

The main thoroughfare linking Waikiki and downtown, Waikiki Road underwent a name change in 1905, when the Territorial Legislature declared it would henceforth be called Kalakaua Avenue. From 1889 to 1903, Hawaiian tramcars plied the road with mule-drawn Victorian-styled carriages. These were replaced by the Honolulu Rapid Transit's electric trolleys. Queen Lili'uokalani's Waikiki home is on the right in this photo and the dowager Queen Kapi'olani's residence, bequeathed to Prince Kuhio upon Lili'uolani's death, is on the right. Kuhio later built his estate, "Pualeilani," on the property. *Baker-Van Dyke Collection*

At his death in 1874, King William Kanaina Lunalilo willed his Waikiki residence to Queen Emma, widow of Alexander Liholiho, King Kamehameha IV. Situated on the *ewa* (west) bank of 'Apuakehau Stream and set back from the foreign socialites' clamor on the beachfront, this modest wooden structure served as a quiet retreat for the dowager Queen and her servants. The International Market Place now sits on this site. *Herman Stolpe, Bishop Museum*

Copious artisian-fed freshwater springs bubbled into pools on the property adjacent to Queen Emma's home. 1870. *Baker-Van Dyke Collection*

Queen Lili'uokalani's pier, built as part of her estate on what is now Kuhio Beach. 1919. *E.H. Dortmund, Bishop Museum*

"Pualeilani," the Waikiki beach residence of Prince Kuhio and his wife. In 1935, the City and County of Honolulu purchased this last royal residence in Waikiki. Victims of a municipal beach improvement program, the home and nearby Lili'uokalani's pier were destroyed. Photo, circa 1905. *Bishop Museum*

PRINCESS KAʻIULANI

A time travel to old Waikiki would not be complete without a final visit—to the ʻAinahau home of Princess Kaʻiulani and her father, Governor Archibald S. Cleghorn. This grand Waikiki estate, which stretched from Kalakaua Avenue at present-day Kaʻiulani Street back to the Ala Wai Canal, was lushly landscaped by the old Governor. An avid botanist who also landscaped ʻIolani Palace and planted the ironwood trees along the Diamond Head end of Kalakaua Avenue, the Governor designed Japanese gardens, verdant walkways, and fern-lined roads at ʻAinahau, transforming the grounds into a serene, natural retreat. Several of the little Princess' favorite bird, the beautiful peacock, strolled about the lawns, perching in the trees and piercing the air with their shrill cry.

The vast lands of ʻAinahau had been acquired by Governor Cleghorn in 1872 for only $300. The grounds were originally used as an ocean retreat by Governor Cleghorn, his wife the Princess Likelike (sister of King Kalakaua and Queen Liliʻuokalani), and their beloved daughter Kaʻiulani. A graceful Victorian home was built on the property near present-day Cleghorn Street. ʻAinahau became renowned for its hospitality, the home being the scene of many royal gatherings and *luʻau*.

One of the most distinguished guests at ʻAinahau was Robert Louis Stevenson. Princess Kaʻiulani was 13 years old, when the world-famous author visited ʻAinahau in 1889. He was so impressed with the young girl that he spent many afternoons with her, sitting under a great banyan tree, telling her stories. When he learned that she was going to go to school in Scotland, he wrote her a little poem in her red-plush album to keep her company on her travels:

> Forth from her land to mine she goes,
> The island maid, the island rose,
> Light of hair and bright of face:
> The daughter of a double race.
> Her islands here, in southern sun
> Shall mourn their Kaiulani gone,
> And I, in her dear banyan shade,
> Look vainly for my little maid.
>
> But our Scots islands far away
> Shall glitter with unwonted day,
> And cast for once their tempests by
> To smile in Kaiulani's eye.

Kaʻiulani passed away at ʻAinahau in 1899, when she was only 24 years old. The night she died, her beloved peacocks screeched wildly.

Since her favorite flower had been the Chinese jasmine, Hawaiians called the flower "pikake" or peacock, in honor of the Princess. Following her death, the peacocks at ʻAinahau were eventually given to the Honolulu Zoo, where possibly many of their descendants still live. Governor Cleghorn died in 1910, his ʻAinahau bestowed to the city of Honolulu for the creation of a Kaʻiulani Park—a legacy which was turned down when the city fathers decided that Waikiki already had enough green space! The old Victorian mansion, converted into a small hotel from 1913 to 1917, would burn down in the 1920s. As for the banyan tree made famous by Robert Louis Stevenson—it remained as one of Waikiki's most popular historic sites until it was cut down in 1949 at the insistence of neighbors who complained that it was a nest for rats. All that today remains of ʻAinahau are the street names—Cleghorn, Kaʻiulani and Tusitala or "storyteller," the Samoan name given to Robert Louis Stevenson.

Daughter of Governor Archibald Cleghorn and Princess Miriam Likelike, the adored Princess Victoria Kaʻiulani died on March 6, 1899, three years after this photo was taken. *Baker-Van Dyke Collection*

Princess Kaʻiulani feeds her pet peacocks near the front steps of the ʻAinahau mansion. The bushy palm in the background makes her look like one of her beloved birds in full plumage display. Circa 1895. *Baker-Van Dyke Collection*

Princess Kaʻiulani, dressed in Victorian flounced white, sits on a bench with her croquet partners beneath her banyan tree at ʻAinahau. Her half-sister, Anne, looks off-camera. Kaʻiulani was designated heir apparent to the throne of Hawaiʻi on March 24, 1891, to follow the reign of Queen Liliʻuokalani. *Walter Giffard, Baker-Van Dyke Collection*

25

"Diamond Head crouches like a headless sphinx with its paws in the sea guarding Honolulu,"
read copy in *Colorful Hawaii*, 1945. This photo was taken in the twenties, when Waikiki had
established itself as a world-class tourist destination. The Moana Hotel, then the island's only
big hostelry outside of downtown Honolulu, boasted a fine dining room on the beach (far
left) and its famous pier. Also visible are the Hustace Villa, Cleghorn and Steiner properties,
and the Waikiki Tavern. The waterfront edifice to the far right is the mansion of James B.
Castle, on the site of the present-day Elks Club and Outrigger Canoe Club. *Baker-Van Dyke
Collection*

Early 1900s

ALONG THE WAY TO WAIKIKI

If tired travelers sought an escape from the hustle and bustle of Honolulu town, they would climb aboard one of the trolley cars, pay the 5-cent fare, and head out to the tranquil countryside—to Waikiki of 10,000 coconut trees, taro farms, fishponds, and brilliant white sands.

As the trolley cars exited the city heading towards Diamond Head, the scenery rapidly changed, as the wide, open plains of Moʻiliʻili's taro and rice farms appeared, extending into Manoa Valley and oceanward to Waikiki. Flowing out of the mountain valleys were several natural river systems that fed into freshwater ponds before they emptied into the sea at several places, including the beach at Kalia (presently the site of the Hilton Hawaiian Village), at Waikiki beach (near the present-day Outrigger Hotel), and Kapiʻolani Park (near the intersection of Kapahulu and Kalakaua Avenues). The waters of Waikiki not only supplied the irrigation for the abundant taro and rice farms, but also fed the ancient and extensive offshore and inland fishponds still visible in the Kalia district. The often-bubbling waters also inspired the ancient Hawaiian name of Waikiki, which means "spouting waters."

The Waikiki waters gave something else to the area in the 1890s—mosquitoes everywhere. Introduced into the Hawaiian Islands early in the 19th century on foreign ships, the mosquito flourished in well-watered areas such as Waikiki. Stinging red ants and centipedes also found the beaches excellent nesting grounds, requiring bathers to vigorously shake their beach towels before daring to dry themselves. Visiting Honolulu in 1866, Mark Twain noticed the town was like the Garden of Eden…"til you got a bite." As far as mosquitoes were concerned, the famous author quipped that while in the Islands, he killed 2,000 mosquitoes with each sitting.

As visitors to old Waikiki disembarked from the trolley in 1890, they were struck by the district's peacefulness. There were few commercial enterprises and, other than the farmers and fishermen, the few residents enjoyed royal status and seclusion.

Electric streetcar service to the beach from Honolulu replaced mule-drawn trolleys in 1903, cutting travel time from 45 to 28 minutes. To attract customers, the transit company opened the Waikiki Aquarium deep in Kapiʻolani Park. The Park quickly became Honolulu's favored playground with its bathhouses, hotel dining rooms, private homes, and acres of open space. Its years as a rural setting for Hawaiian royalty, Chinese farmers, and mansion builders were numbered.

Although tramcars customarily ran individually with one mule, often the Waikiki traffic would demand that two cars be hitched together and drawn by a double team. Shades have been drawn to protect the passengers from the late afternoon sun. 1901. *Emma Rickey, Baker-Van Dyke Collection*

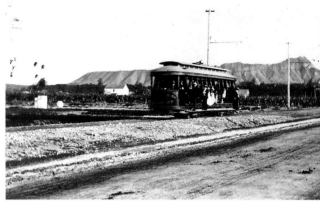

An electric trolley breezes along over the wide-open landscape toward Waikiki. These speedy trolleys cut travel time to the famous beach by at least a third. 1903. *Emma Rickey, Baker-Van Dyke Collection*

Each new trolley could transport up to 56 passengers on double-truck open cars, featuring 14 benches, center aisles, vestibules, running boards, and grab handles. The terminus point, a small trolley house across from the Honolulu Aquarium near Kapi'olani Park, still stands (restored) in 1996. *Baker-Van Dyke Collection*

The properties fronting Waikiki Beach have changed hands and identities several times in the area's long history. During the time of the *ali'i,* the beach was the site of a thriving community. This photo was taken at a period when the modest bathhouses and cabin-style vacation shelters of Honolulu's wealthy lined the sand. This particular structure is the summer bathhouse of W.W. Hall, a merchant and member of the "Honolulu Volunteers," a group of businessmen and citizens who assisted in the overthrow of Queen Lili'uokalani, in an effort to protect "American interests." Circa 1880s. *Baker-Van Dyke Collection*

View looking east from the rooftop garden of the Moana Hotel, across Waikiki's taro patches and waterways toward Punchbowl crater in the distance. Basically, the area of Waikiki behind the beach changed very little from its agricultural use until later in the century. 1903. *Baker-Van Dyke Collection*

Named after Frederick the Great's Potsdam Palace, the Sans Souci ("without care") opened in 1893. The hotel's early claim to fame was that it hosted Robert Louis Stevenson during his second visit to the Islands. Its proprietor, George Lycurgus, was arrested in 1895 for complicity in the royalists' aborted attempt to restore Queen Lili'uokalani to the throne. The 15-story San Souci apartment building occupies the site today. *Bishop Museum*

Waikiki fishermen wait for the next wave to help them push their canoe to higher ground.
The pier in the background, built by developer W.C. Peacock, had just been completed when
this photo was taken in 1890. *Hawai'i State Archives*

This surfer looks out to sea, studying the waters off Waikiki for the perfect wave. At surf spots on these Islands today, surfers still strike a pose much like this, waiting for the next set and checking out the wave size and swell direction. Notice the (now uncommon) seaweed lining the beach and the size and shape of the surfboard. Circa 1899. *Bishop Museum*

A group of fishermen cleaning their nets on the seaweed-cluttered strand. The burgeoning tourist industry would make fishing outriggers, like Waikiki's inland taro patches and rice paddies, a thing of the past. In recent years truckloads of sand, mostly from the dunes of Kahuku, have been brought in to widen the beach and make it more presentable for sunbathers. Early morning beach-sweepers grade the sand in preparation for the daily onslaught of swimmers. Circa 1903. *Baker-Van Dyke Collection*

KAPIʻOLANI PARK

Strolling from Kuhio's home further down Kalakaua Avenue, a time traveler would come to a bridge that spanned the streams that graced Kapiʻolani Park, the 170 acres of greenery established in 1877 and named for King Kalakaua's consort, Queen Kapiʻolani. The park had many islets and waterways surrounded by beautiful gardens, stately ironwood trees, and a mile-long track used for horseracing. Later the Honolulu Aquarium would be established near the park at the end of the trolley line—a notable attraction supported by the trolley company to encourage passengers to take the long ride from town to Waikiki.

A zoo which housed mostly birds was established in 1915 by Ben Hollinger, head of the City and County of Honolulu's park committee.

Diamond Head peeks out over the masterful landscaping of Archibald Cleghorn in Kapiʻolani Park. Circa 1900. *Alonzo Gartley, Bishop Museum*

One of the more interesting features of the park was Makee Island, its encircling placid waterways fed by the Kuʻekaunahi Stream. The Ala Wai Canal drained away the park's water, turning its ponds to muck. This area was later filled in to become the parking lot for the Honolulu Zoo. 1908. *Baker-Van Dyke Collection*

The Honolulu Aquarium opened in March 1904, on land donated by James Castle. His business associate, C.M. Cooke, paid for the construction of this Oriental-style lava rock building, and the Honolulu Rapid Transit Company stocked its tanks with fish. 1918. *Baker-Van Dyke Collection*

Kapiʻolani Park's reflecting pools and lily ponds, like the standing water used to irrigate nearby taro and rice fields, became a breeding ground for mosquitoes. 1908. *Baker-Van Dyke Collection*

Walter F. Dillingham, the fabulously wealthy owner of the Oʻahu Railway and Land Company and Hawaiian Dredging, brought polo to Kapiʻolani Park. The first interisland match pitted Dillingham's Oʻahu "Blues" against Louis von Tempski's Maui "Gold and Blacks" in 1902. The Oʻahu team of A.W. Judd, R.W. Shingle, Dillingham, and C.S. Dole won, claiming the Wichman Cup as their prize. *Baker-Van Dyke Collection*

OLD HOMES

The Kapi'olani Park area was for many years the favored site for the homes of the wealthy elite of the Honolulu business community. The stately homes that once graced the shoreline from the park to Kalehuawehe, the point beyond the present-day Sans Souci Beach, were among the finest in the Territory of Hawai'i. William Irwin of Spreckel's Sugar Company built a Spanish Mission Revival-style mansion in 1899. Twenty-five years later the home was demolished for the construction of an Olympic-sized saltwater pool called the War Memorial Natatorium. Situated at Kalehuawehe Point was the home of James B. Castle of Castle & Cooke. His magnificent multistoried "Kainalu" mansion dominated the beach in front of Diamond Head for many years until the Elks Club razed the old estate to build their modern clubhouse. Next door to the Castle home was the Waikiki estate of the McInerny family. The *hao* tree they used as shade on their *lanai* or porch still graces the outdoor cafe of the New Otani Kaimana Beach Hotel.

From these large, opulent homes on the beach, turn-of-the-century guests could lounge on the *lanai* and watch a favorite Waikiki attraction—surfing. A popular sport in ancient and modern Waikiki, surfing the "bull-mouth monsters" at Waikiki was an exhilarating experience that attracted the attention of one of the greatest American authors—Jack London.

The W.G. Irwin home at Waikiki later became the site of the War Memorial Natatorium. 1908. *Baker-Van Dyke Collection*

The renowned Hustace Villa, Cleghorn beach home, Steiner home, and Waikiki Tavern, in 1915. The Hustace house, adjacent to the Moana Hotel, was used by the hotel as an employees' annex from 1916 to 1950, when it was demolished to build the Surfrider Hotel. *L.E. Edgeworth, Bishop Museum*

The columed entry hall of Samuel B. Castle's Waikiki residence, Kainalu (ocean surf), with its polished ebony banisters, ornate filigree, and marble floor rivaled the finest Honolulu buildings in its opulence and size. *Christian Hedemann, Bishop Museum.*

Once the most conspicuous building along the Diamond Head shoreline, James B. Castle's home "Kainalu" at 2915 Kalakaua Avenue (now the site of the Outrigger Canoe Club and the Elks Club) had beachfront *lanai*s on each of its three principle stories and featured the only privately commissioned Tiffany stained glass windows in Hawai'i. Circa 1905. *Bishop Museum*

JACK LONDON

One of the greatest American authors, Jack London visited Hawai'i several times with his wife, Charmain. The Londons frequently stayed at the Seaside Cottages, the present site of the Royal Hawaiian Hotel. Alexander Hume Ford, a journalist, internationalist, and founder of the Outrigger Canoe Club, encouraged the famed author to write an essay about the Hawaiian sport of surfing to help promote the art around the world. London's essay, "Surfing, the Royal Sport of Waikiki," which is reprinted in *Stories of Hawaii*, is considered one of the best prose descriptions of surfing ever written:

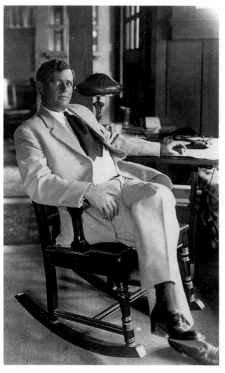

Charmain and Jack London at the Outrigger Canoe Club. 1915. *Baker-Van Dyke Collection*

Jack London at his desk in the Scott cottage on Beachwalk Avenue. 1915. *Baker-Van Dyke Collection*

"And one sits and listens to the perpetual roar, and watches the unending process… tremendous force expressing itself in fury… foam and sound (and) the thought that one may wrestle with this sea raises in ones imagination a thrill of apprehension, almost of fear.

"Why they are a mile long, these bull-mouthed monsters, and they weigh a thousand tons, and they charge in to shore faster than a man can run. What chance? No chance at all is the verdict of the shrinking ego…

"And suddenly, out there where a big smoker lifts skyward, rising like a sea-god from out of the welter of spume and churning white, on the giddy, toppling, overhanging and downfalling, precarious crest appears the dark head of a man. Swiftly he rises through the rushing white… where but a moment before was only the wide desolation and invincible roar, is now a man. Erect, full-statured, not struggling frantically in that wild movement, not buried and crushed and buffeted by those mighty monsters, but standing above them all, calm and superb, posed on the giddy summit, his feet buried in the churning foam, the salt smoke rising to his knees, and all the rest of him in the free air and flashing sunlight, and he is flying through the air, flying forward, flying fast as the surge on which he stands."

On the beach at the Outrigger Canoe Club, the Londons relax with their host Alexander Hume Ford, founder of the club. 1915. *Baker-Van Dyke Collection*

"With smoking crests," one of London's "bull-mouthed monsters" steams towards present-day Queen's beach. Photo, circa 1915. *Bishop Museum*

THE OUTRIGGER
CANOE CLUB

The Outrigger Canoe Club was once a collection of grass houses located on the beach at Waikiki at the present site of the Outrigger Hotel. Alexander Hume Ford started the club in 1908 to revive ancient Hawaiian water sports such as canoeing and surfing, which had begun to decline in popularity. The Hui Nalu o Honolulu (the Surf Club of Honolulu) was one of the many surfing associations begun to encourage beachboys to teach the art of surfing to the visitors. Among the members of the Hui Nalu was a young man who, in July of 1911, was discovered swimming like a fish in Waikiki waters by the Hawai'i representative of the Amateur Athletics Union. When asked his name, the young man simply mumbled, "Duke Kahanamoku." That summer of 1911, a legend was about to be born.

Erosion, probably caused by the newly constructed jetty in the background, has eaten away so much beach frontage that the Outrigger Canoe Club's picket fence, formerly flush with the sand, is now suspended three feet above it. 1918. *L.E. Edgeworth, Bishop Museum*

The Outrigger Canoe Club made canoeing and surfing a prestigious activity, and soon every young socialite wanted lessons in wave riding. 1918. *L.E. Edgeworth, Bishop Museum*

The bathhouse for the Uluniu Women's Swimming Club, an OCC auxiliary. 1910. *Baker-Van Dyke Collection*

The Outrigger Canoe Club's new pavilion, built in 1915, was moved inland in 1925 to make room for the Royal Hawaiian Hotel, then replaced in 1939 with a newer structure, and finally demolished in 1964 for the building of the Outrigger Hotel. Photo, circa 1918. *Baker-Van Dyke Collection*

Is Waikiki the Most Immoral Beach in the World?

As visitors from around the world crowded Waikiki, it acquired a new reputation for sinfulness—especially in terms of the dress of the young women. Acceptable attire in those days necessitated that men and women be properly covered—female bathing suits were cumbersome, full-length gowns which were nearly impossible to swim in. Some of the daring women often doffed the gowns once they were in the water, placing their garments on a bathing platform or at the end of one of the piers that extended into the bay. Underneath they wore a man's bathing suit, which consisted of shorts and a tank top. As long as no one saw them, there was no trouble. After swimming, the young ladies would then retrieve their gowns and exit the water in complete modesty.

Occasionally there were problems with this arrangement. In 1913 several young women returned to the pier to discover that a Good Samaritan had gathered up the abandoned gowns and returned them to the hotel as lost items. With the ocean currents pulling them to sea, the embarrassed ladies had to swim to shore, revealing their bare arms and legs to the shocked and outraged onlookers. With this type of scandalous public indecency taking place in Waikiki, the city of Honolulu considered an ordinance barring women from wearing men's bathing suits. One week later, the idea was dropped after the women of Honolulu let it be known that they would not be dictated to concerning their beachwear fashion. Women in tight-fitting men's bathing suits then became a familiar sight on the beach now known as "Flapper's Acre."

However, the conservative, church-going Hawaiian community was not about to allow the liberality of the female visitor at Waikiki Beach to debase their public modesty. During a 1915 reenactment of an ancient Hawaiian pageant at Waikiki, all of the Hawaiian male warriors wore long underwear dyed the color of flesh to conceal their bare legs, arms, and chests! Was Waikiki becoming the most immoral place in the world by the 1920s? The beachgoers on "Flapper's Acre" were engaging in behavior that shocked conservative Honolulu, including wearing their bathing suits on Waikiki streets! In 1921, the Desha Bathing Suit Act was passed, prohibiting anyone over the age of 14 from wearing bathing suits on Honolulu's streets. That law was on the books until 1949, although it was rarely enforced.

Waikiki regattas drew hundreds of onlookers. Visitors and residents would come together to watch or take part in the thrill of competition. The tradition of watersports events continues today. Events including roughwater swimming, paddling, surfing, and triathalons attract athletic participants and audiences alike. 1914. *Hawai'i State Archives.*

A fashionable flapper in "Roaring Twenties" daring attire, on the beach at Waikiki, 1920s. At least her ankles are covered. *Baker-Van Dyke Collection*

The city staged a reenactment of the landing of Kamehameha the Great at Waikiki Beach. This first pageant, which fostered the annual Kamehameha Day celebrations, was hampered by the morality laws of the 1910s which declared that "showing of unclad skin on the beach is immoral." Each of the participants in this terribly hot noon-time performance was forced to wear "badly dyed long drawers and long-sleeved undershirts." Hula girls sweltered in below-the-knees leggings and grass shirts, and the young men, dressed in brown-dyed union suits, toiled through their dance routines and marches. *Baker-Van Dyke Collection*

The Royal Hawaiian and Moana Hotels, 1930. A trolley moves along Kalakaua Avenue in front of the Cleghorn beach house. Already the bungalow-style houses that would so characterize Waikiki's neighborhoods have begun to proliferate on the *mauka* side of the street. These quaint cottages would eventually disappear, casualties of the high-rise construction frenzy that swept through Waikiki in the sixties and seventies. *Baker-Van Dyke Collection*

The Grand Hotels

With the fame of Waikiki growing after the turn of the century, prospects for establishing commercial hotels seemed more viable. A few visitor accommodations had been opened before 1900, but they were largely unsuccessful in their attempts to attract business to the remote district. The Park Beach Hotel near Kapi'olani Park, for example, in 1888 was the earliest hotel in Waikiki. A year later the establishment closed due to lack of business. After the aborted 1895 revolution temporarily closed the doors of Lycurgus' Sans Souci, the hotel reopened under the management of Alexander Hawes. However, in a few years, Hawes converted the hotel into a private residence.

The only successful commercial businesses in 19th-century Waikiki were the bathhouses, which offered facilities for daytime visitors to the beach. The Occidental Bathhouse, the Waikiki Villa, and the Long Branch Baths were early such establishments located on the beach between the present-day Sheraton Waikiki Hotel and the Outrigger Hotel. The proprietor of the Long Branch Baths was Jim Dodd, the owner of the Pantheon Saloon in downtown Honolulu; he provided his saloon patrons with a private tramway service to his Waikiki bathhouse. For their amusement, Dodd, a former circus performer, installed the Waikiki "marine toboggan" run, a long, wooden ramp 40 feet high, where the adventurous would be propelled on wooden planks across Waikiki bay like skipping stones!

The establishment of a commercially successful hotel in Waikiki was the dream of businessman W.C. Peacock, who on March 11, 1901 opened the "First Lady of Waikiki," the Moana Hotel, on the site of the old royal compound of Ulukou. Designed by island architect O.G. Traphagen, the Moana Hotel was the tallest building in the islands when it opened its doors, affording from its top floor an unparalleled view of the leeward coast of O'ahu. So tall was the building that on August 11, 1910 the captain of the British barkentine *Helga* mistook the lights in the rooftop for a lighthouse. Using the hotel's position to navigate the coast, the *Helga* hit Waikiki reef, making the Moana possibly the only hotel in the world to have sunk a ship!

As more and more visitors stayed in Waikiki at the Moana, other hotels followed, including the Waikiki Inn, Seaside Cottages, Cassidy's At the Beach or Gray's By-the-Sea.

Occidental Hotel at Waikiki, 1880. Several such cottage-style retreats came into existence in the area near the turn of the century. Wealthy families and members of the Hawaiian *ali'i*, used these cabanas as changing rooms and shelters for the long, relaxing days on the beach. The little Victorian summer cottages were "sparsely" furnished according to the brocade-tapestry style of the day. They were all supplanted by bigger hotels. *Bishop Museum*

Waikiki Beach in 1935, with the two hotels that would dominate the scene into the sixties. From left to right: the beachfront house of Miss Bertha Young, whose father built the downtown Alexander Young Hotel; the Royal Hawaiian Hotel; the Outrigger Canoe Club (beneath the trees); the Hui Nalu Beach Boys Club, which counted Duke Kahanamoku among its members; the Moana Hotel's on-the-water restaurant and its expanded high-rise; the distinctive turreted house of Frank Hustace, the Cleghorn beach house, and the James Steiner residence. *Bishop Museum*

Near the site of the future Moana Hotel stood the Long Branch Baths, a series of bathhouses and a toboggan slide. Skilled riders of the slide could skip out over the water for a hundred feet and more. 1892. *Bishop Museum*

The view toward Diamond Head from the beach fronting the Royal Hawaiian Hotel, in 1929. The canoe has just been launched from the Outrigger Canoe Club, its sail newly deployed by an overly optimistic crew on this windless afternoon. One of the new biplanes of the Army Air Corps flies over the scene. (Compare this photo to the Burgess lithograph on pp. 2-3). *Baker-Van Dyke Collection*

THE MOANA

Waikiki's First "Ultra-Modern" Hotel

It all started on March 11, 1901, when a brand-new, four-story, 75-room Moana Hotel welcomed its first guests—a convention of 100 Shriners from California.

The "ultra-modern" wooden edifice, the biggest thing between Diamond Head and Honolulu Harbor, shouldered above the big private homes next door and dominated the beach. But it was lovely—a rustic, lodge-like idea from the 19th century with white woodwork, airy porches and a graceful, dormer roof line.

Inside were all the latest conveniences—an elevator, a private bath for each room, brass bedsteads, marble washstands, telephones, and electric lights. Waikiki had never seen anything like it. Finally, after years of short-lived cottage-style accommodations or no guest facilities at all, the beach had a respectable hostelry. Waikiki suddenly was a resort.

Fifteen years after its opening, the Moana Hotel added 100 new rooms in two wings, creating a lovely courtyard facing the sea. The Moana's great banyan tree sheltered the courtyard and crowds of dancers moved to the swinging sounds of the Moana Hotel Orchestra and its innovative band leader, Johnny Noble. By 1920, the rhythms were jazzy and getting faster.

The Moana, from across the street at the corner of Ka'iulani and Kalakaua Avenues. 1950. *Baker-Van Dyke Collection*

The Moana Hotel in 1920. The expansive lawn in the foreground led to the newly constructed Moana Cottages, which were replaced by the Princes Kaʻiulani Hotel in June 1955. The two new concrete wings, completed in 1918 and costing $530,000, more than doubled the hotel's capacity. The sixth-story walkway joining the wings to the roof-top garden was the newest addition to the edifice. *Baker-Van Dyke Collection*

SEASIDE AND HALEKULANI HOTELS

The former royal compound under the co-conuts at Helumoa, down the beach from the Moana Hotel, was purchased by George Macfarlane, a Scottish businessman who had been involved in Honolulu hotels since 1888. He assembled a group of substantial cottages on the site and launched the Seaside Hotel in 1906.

By the mere fact of its strategic and historic location under one of Hawai'i's most beautiful coconut groves, the Seaside was a special garden spot, much beloved by residents and visitors alike. Alice Roosevelt, irrepressible daughter of President Teddy Roosevelt, visited the Seaside twice, the second time with her new husband, Nicholas Longworth. Notoriously unconventional, Alice shocked Honolulu's fawning socialites when she smoked in public. In 1925 the cottages were razed or moved to construct the Royal Hawaiian Hotel.

Next door to the Seaside, another early player in the effort to attract first-class travelers was the Halekulani Hotel, stitched together from several beach properties in 1917. The understated, casual resort with a famous hau tree *lanai* had a long life as Waikiki's best-loved "cottage hotel." Its most important contribution to the culture of Waikiki may have been its constant faith in local Hawaiian music which the Kimball family, the hotel's long-time owners, loved. Over the years they gave hundreds of local singers and musicians the chance to perform on the Halekulani's oceanside *lanai*. The Halekulani, "house befitting heaven," finally surrendered to real-estate realities in 1980. New Japanese owners replaced the hotel's bungalows with high-rise towers.

Hau Tree Lanai at the Halekulani Hotel, 1919. The hau, a lowland tree of the hibiscus variety, could be trained on trellises to form a tangled, curling-branched roof. *Baker-Van Dyke Collection*

With its wrap-around verandah and high-roofed Victorian turret, this cottage, often referred to as "the Longworth cottage," was the largest at the Seaside Hotel. Nicholas Longworth and his wife, Alice Roosevelt, daughter of President Teddy Roosevelt, stayed here. This Ray Jerome Baker photo turned into a postcard. Circa 1908. *Baker-Van Dyke Collection*

The famous Seaside Hotel beachfront dining room quickly became the Waikiki socialites' favorite venue for Sunday afternoon gatherings. Circa 1910. *J.A. Gonsalves Collection, Bishop Museum*

NIUMALU HOTEL: SITE OF THE FUTURE HILTON HAWAIIAN VILLAGE

The Heen Investment Company purchased the Pierpoint Hotel and its neighbors Hummel's Court and Cressaty's Court in 1926. The existing cottages were refurbished and the six acres of property relandscaped before the hotel owners renamed it, the Niumalu (Sheltering Palms). A number of new structures were built to accomodate up to 125 guests with a dining room and dance floor in the central complex. Originally the site of the John Ena home on Kalia Road, the Niumalu Hotel was eventually replaced by the world-class Hilton Hawaiian Village. Circa 1932. *Baker-Van Dyke Collection*

The western-most end of Waikiki Beach, the future site of the Hilton Hawaiian Village. 1920. *Baker-Van Dyke Collection*

DRAINING OF THE ALA WAI CANAL

Before the grand hotels of Waikiki could ever be built, the rice paddies, ancient fishponds, taro fields, and marshes which dominated the district needed to be drained. The growth of tourism required dry real estate, a promise fulfilled by the dredging of the Ala Wai Canal.

Streams from three great Ko'olau mountain valleys drained into a flood plain behind Waikiki, finally reaching the sea by three different outlets through the sand at Waikiki. Development along the beach had dammed some of this natural drainage, creating backwaters of stagnant swamp—breeding grounds for mosquitoes. During heavy rains, Waikiki became a giant mudflat.

As early as 1906, health officials had called for dredging a canal to drain the streams away from Waikiki. Under the efforts of Territorial Governor Lucius E. Pinkham, 161 acres of land were procured by the Territory and $100,000 appropriated for the Waikiki reclamation project. The dredging began in 1921 by the Hawaiian Dredging Company, the early fill used to build up the land by the current McKinley High School. The project was finished by 1924, although expansion of the waterway would continue until 1928.

Waikiki had been changed forever by the Ala Wai Canal. The ancient irrigation systems were gone, the farms were gone, the streams were gone, the mosquitoes were gone, and Waikiki was separated from the rest of Honolulu by a broad canal. On the new, high-and-dry lands behind the hotels, developers laid out tracts of inexpensive homes and garden apartments. Almost overnight Waikiki became urban.

An amusement park near Fort DeRussy proved Waikiki's capacity for big crowds. Drive-in burger stands and movie theaters opened along Kalakaua Avenue. Curio shops and restaurants set up business on the reclaimed land behind the beach. The Mossman family opened Lalani Village near Kapi'olani Park, where visitors were invited to learn about traditional Hawaiian life. Kuluwaimaka, court chanter during the reign of King David Kalakaua, provided the village and its guests with his priceless *mana'o*, "knowledge of the old," rapidly disappearing ways.

At the bridge on Ala Moana looking towards St. Louis and Maunalani Heights, 1945. To the left is the automobile repair shop of Murphy-Aloha Motors, dealers of Oldsmobile and Chevrolet cars. After the April 1, 1946 tidal wave, boats were no longer allowed mooring space on the Ala Wai Canal. Today, Hawai'i's new convention center rises in the Aloha Motors area. *Baker-Van Dyke Collection*

The Royal opened on February 1, 1927 with a series of parties, the likes of which Hawai'i had never seen before, or since. Very much a product of Roaring Twenties' sensibilities, the Pink Palace offered a more avante garde approach to the hostelry business. While its neighbor, the Moana, clung to an image of Victorian conservatism, the Royal presaged the glitzy flash and accelerated hoopla that became Waikiki's hallmark. *Baker-Van Dyke Collection*

THE ROYAL HAWAIIAN
The "Royal"

Matson Navigation Company decided travelers to Hawai'i needed first-class accommodation and in 1925 commissioned the construction of *Malolo*, a 650-passenger luxury liner capable of 22 knots, shortening the six-and-a-half-day San Francisco-Honolulu trip by two days. The same year, the old Seaside Hotel closed and ground was broken for the Royal Hawaiian Hotel. The "Pink Palace," the "Queen of the Pacific," was destined to become one of the great resort hotels in the world.

After the biggest party Hawai'i had ever seen, the $5 million California mission-inspired hotel on February 1, 1927 opened its 400 rooms to the world's most discriminating travelers. They arrived with their own automobiles and with truckloads of luggage. Rockefellers, Fords, Du Ponts and more pedestrian millionaires usually stayed more than a month, spending $14 per night (vs. $8 at the Moana next door). They played golf on a new course set out for them at Kahala Beach on the other side of Diamond Head, not far from the pig farms of Wai'alae.

Now Waikiki had two "big" hotels and a few established tropical hideaways lined up on its busy beach. Visitors wanted to learn how to surf. They wanted to take a ride in a canoe. They wanted to see the "hula-hula."

Brawny locals obliged them with friendly smiles and legendary aloha. Beachboys became sunny celebrities when sweethearts Mary Pickford and Douglas Fairbanks posed with them for *Photoplay* magazine. Duke Kahanamoku, 1912 Olympic swimming champion and all-around waterman, became Hawai'i's goodwill ambassador. Wherever he went, he spread the good news about surfing, Hawai'i, and Waikiki's golden charms.

An early aerial view of the Royal Hawaiian Hotel. 1929. *Baker-Van Dyke Collection*

Opening night at the Royal Hawaiian Hotel, February 1, 1927. The room was filled with the social elite of Hawai'i. Seated at the table at the bottom center were Princess Elizabeth Kahanu, widow of Prince Kuhio and now Mrs. Frank Woods; Senator Charles Chillingworth and Mrs. Chillingworth; Mr. and Mrs. Beckley; and Frank Woods. *Baker-Van Dyke Collection*

PROMOTING PARADISE

Once built, Waikiki's hotels needed to keep their rooms full. The Hawai'i Promotion Committee began with a taxpayer-funded budget of $3,600 to distribute brochures at the St. Louis World's Fair in 1903. The group later became the Hawai'i Tourist Bureau, now called the Hawai'i *Visitors* Bureau, with an annual budget of over $15 million.

Jack London helped with articles for mainland newspapers and magazines, including one titled *A Royal Sport: Surfing at Waikiki*. He had been introduced to the sport by George Freeth and Alexander Hume Ford, founders of Waikiki's then informal club for watermen, the Outrigger Canoe Club.

Waikiki's allure got a big boost in 1915, when "On the Beach at Waikiki," sung first at the Panama-Pacific Exposition in San Francisco, became a hit all across the country. The printed descriptions were now reinforced by the sweet rhythms of popular Hawaiian songs.

Fanciful sheet-music illustrations for songs like "Waikiki Mermaid," "Hula Blues," and "Wicky Wacky Woo" added seductive visuals. Typical scenes included Diamond Head's silhouette, palm trees, moonlight tracing a silvery path on the calm Pacific, a hula maiden, or a pair of young lovers. Waikiki had entered the American consciousness as the ultimate romantic serenade.

Lyrics from a popular Hawaiian song, "...*YOUR TROPIC NIGHTS AND WONDERFUL CHARMS*" evoked a certain nostalgia for the Waikiki of old.

Among the many singers who interpreted this favorite was a Chinese-Hawaiian crooner named Don Ho. He started his career at Honey's, a Kailua bar owned by his mother. In the mid-sixties he moved to the old "Duke Kahanamoku's" nightclub in the International Market Place, propelled by wonderful songs written by his friend, Kui Lee. Songs like "I'll Remember You," "Lahainaluna," and "One Paddle, Two Paddle" made Don Ho a household name and gave Hawaiian music its first fresh sound since "Little Grass Shack."

From 1907 to 1916 Hawai'i celebrated an annual mid-winter carnival season in February. The Kamehameha Day pageants became such a hit after their debut in 1916 that they replaced the carnival with the annual June 11 holiday, Kamehameha Day. *Baker-Van Dyke Collection*

The singers and dancers of the Royal Hawaiian Hotel Glee Club began entertaining tourists at Kapi'olani Park in 1934 at the weekly Kodak Hula Show. The show has been a popular Waikiki attraction ever since. *Baker-Van Dyke Collection*

SEE HAWAII

MATSON NAVIGATION CO.
SAN FRANCISCO — HONOLULU
DIRECT TO VOLCANO

An early colorful advertisement to attract visitors to Hawai'i. 1918. *Baker-Van Dyke Collection*

Steamer Day, Honolulu.

Boat Day in Honolulu, 1918. Whenever Matson's big liners arrived or departed Honolulu Harbor it was a festive event, with Hawaiian singers strumming their ukuleles, multicolored streamers flying from the deck, and leis tossed into the boat's wake. *Baker-Van Dyke Collection*

A view of Manoa Valley, Palolo Valley, and Waikiki. By the 1950s Waikiki's streams and ponds had been filled in with ground dredged in the making of the Ala Wai Canal. A new municipal golf course had replaced the wetland agriculture, the Moana had added the Surfrider Hotel to its property, and the Royal had just celebrated its silver anniversary. From the agricultural lifestyle and communal living of the ancient Hawaiians, to the starched and proper days of the monarchy and Protestant missionaries, to the loose flappers of the Roaring Twenties, and on into the age of materialism, the history and attitudinal changes in Hawai'i have been played out on this stretch of beach. Except for a few man-made structures, this photo could have been taken a century ago (if cameras existed). *Baker-Van Dyke Collection*

Rice paddies glisten in the sunlight like a missionary patchwork quilt in one of the first aerial photos of the Waikiki resort area, prior to construction of the Ala Wai Canal. Thriving taro patches add a striped texture to this photo. Kalakaua Avenue cuts horizontally through the growing residential neighborhoods, bridges the broad *muliwai* (estuary) of ʻApuakehau Stream, and bends along the shores of Waikiki. Notice the jetty and pier and the Moana Hotel with its new concrete wings. The Kalia fishponds appear, extreme left. 1920. *Baker-Van Dyke Collection.*

From the peak of Diamond Head in 1890, Kapiʻolani Park and Waikiki seem dominated by the immense race track that served as a playground for the wealthy residents of Honolulu. In the distance is the shadowed mound of Punchbowl crater, and the sparsely populated coastline of Honolulu. *Bishop Museum*

By 1930, Waikiki had become a mecca for movie stars. Here, a crowd gathers to watch the filming of a motion picture on the beach of the Royal Hawaiian Hotel. 1929. *Baker-Van Dyke Collection*

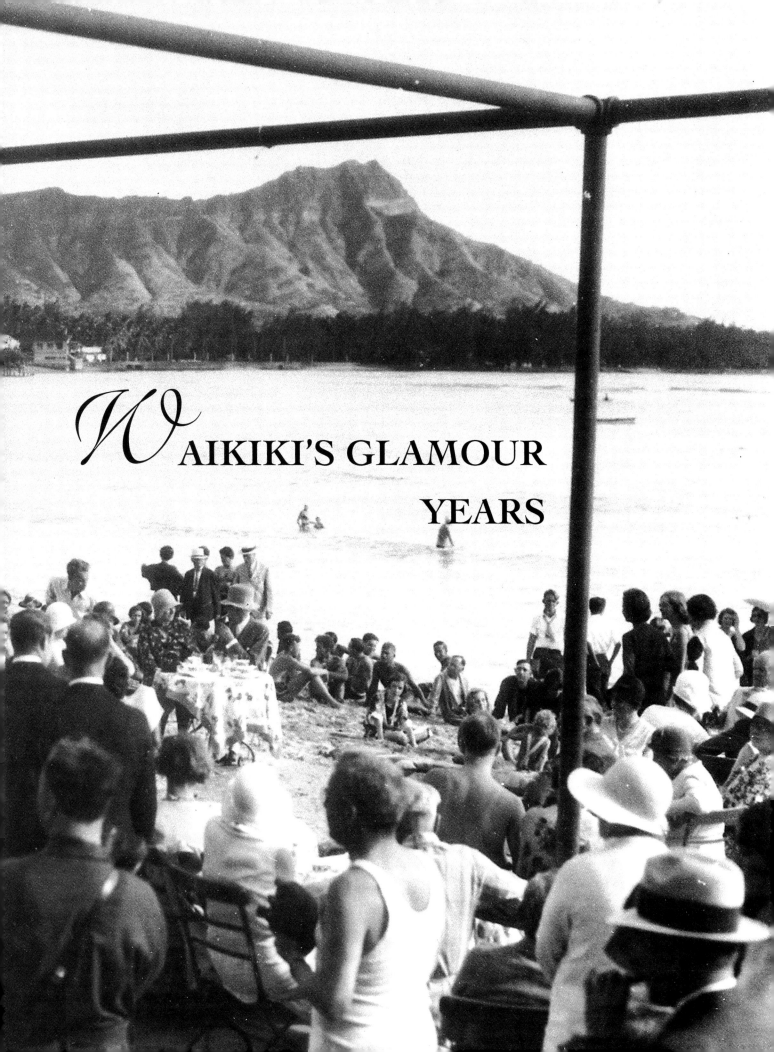

Waikiki's Glamour Years

The year the Royal Hawaiian Hotel opened, Mrs. Cassidy's boarding house (where the Hilton Hawaiian Village is now located; $60 per month including meals) was replaced by the graceful cottage-style Niumalu ("sheltering palms") Hotel. The Niumalu and the new main building at the Halekulani typified the gracious *kama'aina* architectural style, with sloping, double-pitched hip roof lines, lava-rock walls, and cool, spacious rooms. Possibly the best evidence of Waikiki's new-found classiness was the 1929 arrival of San Francisco's prestigious Gump's specialty store, erecting a graceful blue-tile-roofed building on the corner of Kalakaua Avenue at Lewers Street (this landmark now houses a fast-food outlet).

The dream of a "Golden Age" in Hawai'i tourism at the end of the 1920s came to a startling end on Black Tuesday, October 29, 1929. The "Great Crash" hit Waikiki hard. Visitor counts dropped from 22,000 in 1929 to 10,000 in 1932. There were bankruptcies and failures in the pineapple business, and real-estate sales came to a standstill. The Niumalu Hotel was sold at public auction and the Halekulani couldn't meet its payroll. "There were no tourists anywhere," said one hotelier.

The bigger hotels managed to survive, and by 1935 visitor counts began to increase. President Franklin Delano Roosevelt visited the Hawaiian Islands, his sons surfing with Duke Kahanamoku at Waikiki Beach. Other famous visitors included Shirley Temple, Babe Ruth, Charlie Chaplin, George Bernard Shaw, Carole Lombard, Bing Crosby, Spencer Tracy, George and Gracie Allen, and Groucho Marx. Millionaire industrialists again spent months at the Royal. Doris Duke, one of America's richest and most publicized young women, became a regular, surfing with her beachboy pals. In 1935, "Hawaii Calls" began its seductive radio broadcasts from the Banyan Court at the Moana Hotel, bringing the sounds of Hawaiian music into homes across the nation every Saturday evening for over 30 years.

The decade of the 1930s was Waikiki's most famous era. These were the years when ships arrived in Honolulu at Aloha Tower on Boat Day to the romantic strains of the Royal Hawaiian Band and the colorful streamers thrown on the ship by throngs of well-wishers. Escorted to their Waikiki hotels in taxies or private limousines, visitors freely mixed with local residents in an ambiance filled with steel guitar melodies enjoyed under tropical moonlight. Although Waikiki was a world-famous visitor destination, it remained distinctly a local residential district so that hotels and commercial tour activities blended with little "mama and papa-san" stores, laundries, soda fountains, and children of all races enjoying the beaches.

Yet, even in the midst of this Pacific idyll, the clouds of war were brewing on the horizon. Europe was by 1939 engulfed in war, and news of Japan's militarism in China dampened the enthusiasms of the traditional, well-heeled traveler. Military uniforms became more common in Waikiki's hotel lobbies and lounges. Diamond Head itself had been purchased by the U.S. military, and crews spent the late 1930s turning the strategic promontory into an ant hill of tunnels, bunkers, gun turrets, and transmitters. As a Japanese midget submarine surveyed the coast of Waikiki in the late evening of December 6, 1941, the crew could hear the distant sounds of the band of the Royal Hawaiian Hotel serenading the last dance before the days of war.

The most famous man in the world in his day, the Prince of Wales, learns to ride an outrigger canoe at the Moana Hotel in 1920. In January 1936 he became King Edward VIII, but he abdicated his throne in December 1936. *Baker-Van Dyke Collection*

Famous Hollywood actor and comedian Charlie Chaplin poses with hula girls. 1915. *U. Teragawachi, Bishop Museum*

Bing Crosby rides a scooter in front of the Royal Hawaiian Hotel, taking a break in shooting the film *Waikiki Wedding.* 1935. *Tai Sing Loo Collection, Bishop Museum*

Queen Lili'uokalani's pier, in the middle distance off Kuhio Beach, and the famed Moana pier. 1930. Both would soon be removed. *Baker-Van Dyke Collection*

Paddle crews and their spectators throng the beach in front of the Outrigger Canoe Club at the finish line of an outrigger canoe race. Such regattas became a mainstay of Waikiki Beach activities, attracting rival canoe clubs from all over the Islands. Today, the Outrigger Canoe Club holds numerous paddleboard and single-man outrigger canoe regattas, and sponsors top-ranking open-ocean paddling teams. Circa 1920. *Bishop Museum*

Duke Kahanamoku and the Beachboys

Duke Kahanamoku was the eldest son of Honolulu Sheriff Duke Kahanamoku. The young Duke was raised in the Kalia fishing village at the current site of the Hilton Hawaiian Village Hotel. Attending Waikiki School, the young Hawaiian more often found himself swimming in the ocean than attending classes. When he was "discovered" in 1911, the AAU official asked the young man to be formally timed in the 100-meter freestyle swim. The whole town came out to watch as Duke was clocked in Honolulu Harbor breaking the world's record. The time was sent to New York City, where AAU officials refused to accept the new world record—"Hawaiian judges are advised to use stopwatches, not alarm clock," they are reported to have told the Honolulu officials. No one could possibly swim that fast.

Joining the U.S. Olympic swim team, Duke Kahanamoku proved in 1912 at Stockholm, Sweden, that he was the fastest swimmer in the world. Winning gold medals for the United States in the 100- and 400-meter freestyle swim, he returned to the Islands as Hawai'i's first Olympic medalist and an embodiment of Hawaiian pride. Duke would repeat his "gold" victory in the 1920 Olympics. In his mid-thirties, he vied again for the gold during the 1924 Olympics. Disappointed, he captured the silver medal. He later remarked that he didn't feel so bad losing—"they put Tarzan up against me." The future Tarzan of the movies, Johnny Weissmuller, beat Duke in 1924. In 1927, the two friends helped to dedicate the Natatorium—they were joined by island swimmer Clarence "Buster" Crabbe, destined to be another Tarzan in the movies.

Always a modest, quiet man whose head was never turned by his fame as a swimmer, surfer, and Hollywood actor, Duke Kahanamoku was a Hawaiian traditionalist. He preferred to surf with his solid koa wood surfboard, which weighed over 150 pounds, declining to use the lighter "hollow boards." When other beachboys would slim their boards to make them smaller and faster, Kahanamoku would still use the larger boards. Once his friend "Mongoose" slimmed his board down— Duke never said a word in protest. However, later when Mongoose came back to the beach, he found that Duke had sawed off the nose of his lighter board! Mongoose never again tried to slim his boards down—at least not in Duke's presence.

With the fame of Duke Kahanamoku extending around the world, the notoriety of the Hawaiian beachboy as Waikiki's ambassador of aloha soon followed. Visitors to the Islands would be welcomed on the beach by these young Hawaiian men, who would teach them to surf, thrill them with canoe rides, or even guide them about the island. Hollywood movie stars such as Cary Grant, Spencer Tracy and little Shirley Temple were regaled by the beachboys, as were the sons of President Franklin Roosevelt during his 1934 visit to O'ahu. Legends among the beachboys included "Chick" Daniels, "Panama" Dave, Scooter Boy, Steamboat, Blue Makua, and the surfing dog "Night Hawk." The most famous of the Hawaiian surfers, however, remained Duke, who in his long career as the Sheriff of Honolulu was also the "official greeter" of the Hawaiian Islands. When he passed away in 1969, thousands of mourners gathered on Waikiki Beach to watch his ashes scattered into the ocean which he so loved. One newspaper referred to the solemn event as the last royal funeral to have taken place in Hawai'i.

Duke Kahanamoku and Norman Ross pose as if they are about to start a swimming race, in front of the Moana Hotel. 1915. *Baker-Van Dyke Collection*

Duke Kahanamoku teaches a group of Army nurses to ride an outrigger canoe. Although he became an internationally known celebrity, Duke never lost the graciousness and amiability that made him such a beloved representative of the aloha spirit. 1949. *Baker-Van Dyke Collection*

Duke Kahanamoku shares a pineapple with Amelia Earhart at Waikiki. 1935. *Baker-Van Dyke Collection*

The Waikiki Beach Patrol at its headquarters near the Royal Hawaiian Hotel. They served as lifeguards and taught outrigger canoe paddling, surfing, and swimming. 1935. *Bishop Museum*

Duke charges into a graceful take-off on a Waikiki comber. One day, in rare 15-to-20-foot storm-generated surf, Duke rode a wave from the outermost reef to Waikiki Beach, a record distance of a mile. Since the filling in of Ku'ekaunahi Stream changed the bottom configuration of the bay, such long waves have disappeared. *Bishop Museum*

Duke Kahanamoku at the Outrigger Canoe Club. This photo influenced sculptor Jan Fisher in his treatment of Duke for the statue that now stands at Kuhio Beach in Waikiki. 1915. *Baker-Van Dyke Collection*

From left to right: L.P. Thurston, George "Dad" Center, unidentified, Douglas Fairbanks, Mary Pickford, and Duke Kahanamoku, 1929. In the past decades, well-dressed visitors graced Waikiki's boulevards, hotels, and restaurants wearing coats and ties. Today, the only suits you'll find in Waikiki are scanty bathing suits. The dress code in Waikiki is so relaxed that signs outside restaurants and hotel lobbies read, "Footwear and shirts must be worn." *Tai Sing Loo, Bishop Museum*

Notable beachboys in Waikiki dressed for a Halekulani show. *Baker-Van Dyke Collection*

Waikiki's most famous beachboys of the 1920s. *Baker-Van Dyke Collection*

In 1925 the Irwin house was torn down to erect the War Memorial Natatorium, as a monument to honor those killed in World War I. Many believed, however, it was built to honor the considerable achievements of Duke Kahanamoku. He was on hand for the official opening of the facility on August 24, 1927. Advertised as "the only saltwater swimming pool in the world," it soon became an engineering debacle as migrating sand clogged its circulation system. Community leaders have argued for decades about what to do. Meanwhile, the closed Natatorium still stands, a reminder of Waikiki's glamorous past. *Hawai'i State Archives*

Canoes on the beach at Waikiki, 1926. In those days, the canoes were hollowed-out logs of koa wood, with outriggers made from *hau*. Today's sleek models are mostly fiberglass. *Baker-Van Dyke Collection*

Duke Kahanamoku and 14-year-old Marston Campbell were well known at the Outrigger Canoe Club for creative tandem-surfing tricks. 1910. *Baker-Van Dyke Collection*

Children play outside their home on Hobron Lane and Ena Road. 1933. *Baker-Van Dyke Collection*

House on Hobron Lane, 1933. The architectural revolution that changed the appearance of Waikiki saw these little plantation-style houses disappear soon after the last grass shacks. Mansions made way for hotels. A few bungalows like the one below still survive, hemmed in by high-rises. *Baker-Van Dyke Collection*

The "Camel Bell," a dress shop and Chinese gift shop on Lewers Street run by world-famous Chinese traveler Dorothy Tru Bell. The neighborhood between Kalakaua and the Ala Wai, which came to be known as "The Jungle" in the sixties and seventies, housed bohemians, surfers, and hippies in doomed, dilapidated cottages. These were bulldozed to build apartment buildings and low-rate, off-the-beach hotels. *Baker-Van Dyke Collection*

Kapiʻolani Boulevard and Pensacola Street, an area technically in the Waikiki district. 1932. *Baker-Van Dyke Collection*

In the 1930s, the South Seas was a very popular restaurant and night club on Kalakaua Avenue. With thatched roof, indoor-outdoor dining, and a delightful Polynesian ambiance, it offered locals and tourists a romantic and relaxed Island-style experience. *Baker-Van Dyke Collection*

The dining room of the Moana Hotel hung out over the beach. Beneath it were the men's and women's changing rooms, showers, and lockers. Privileged beachgoers lounge in the shade of hotel-issued umbrellas. 1938. *Baker-Van Dyke Collection*

The beach in front of the Outrigger Canoe Club, looking toward the Ala Moana Hotel and its dining room. The landmark Moana pier no longer stands. 1938. *Baker-Van Dyke Collection*

Lewers Road at Kalia, Waikiki, 1937. So much has been made in recent years of the loss of thousands of Waikiki palms, that the local community association has sponsored a tree-planting program. *Bishop Museum*

Stores along Ena Road near Hobron Lane. 1930. *Baker-Van Dyke Collection*

Kalakaua Avenue and Beachwalk, 1935. Remembered well were Ansteth's and Sutherland's Ice Cream. Planet Hollywood now sits on the site. *Baker-Van Dyke Collection*

After seating theater guests in rows of plush velvet seats, the usherettes of the Waikiki Theater went up on stage in front of the movie screen and entertained their guests with hulas danced to the music of the theater organ. *Baker-Van Dyke Collection*

Designed by C.W. Dickey, the Waikiki
Theater opened on August 20, 1936, showing
Under Two Flags, starring Claudette Colbert,
Ronald Colman, and Rosalind Russell.
Theatergoers were treated to a magical
interior. Lining the walls were tropical
plants created from papier-mache by the
artist Homer Merrill. Included in this
florascape were banana trees, *hala,* papaya,
night-blooming cereus, ti leaf, and ferns.
When the lights dimmed, the ceiling filled
with projected stars and moonlit clouds that
swirled. *Baker-Van Dyke Collection*

Baker-Van Dyke Collection

WORLD WAR II

As huge black clouds rose in the west over Pearl Harbor on the morning of December 7, 1941, Waikiki effectively shut down as a vacation spot. Between 1942 and 1945, an estimated one million military and civilian personnel passed through the Islands, most of them having "R & R" leave in Waikiki. The Matson fleet of white passenger liners became troop carriers. All the major hotels were taken over by the military—the Royal Hawaiian being the exclusive retreat for submarine crews, and the Moana used by the Navy. Army personnel stayed at the Breakers Hotel.

Fear of full-scale Japanese invasion forced curfews and strict blackouts. A bramble of barbed wire stretched the length of Waikiki. The local monthly *Paradise of the Pacific* admitted that "instead of being a remote lotus land for tourists, Hawaii finds herself a center of world-shaping events…The islands have renounced holiday celebration for the duration."

Still, amid the grim, life-and-death dramas of wartime, Waikiki's bars, beaches, and dance floors were places to let off steam, find romance, and have a good laugh. With recreation centers, bars, tattoo parlors, and even a few brothels, Waikiki had entered its "honky-tonk" years. The carousing and torrid affairs of America's fighting men added a lusty, heroic coloring to the district. After the war, the servicemen were sent home with parades, lei, and smiles, to tell their friends about Waikiki's hospitality and fine weather. Some decided to stay. Others were to eventually return.

During the war, the Moana and Royal Hawaiian Hotels became "rest and recreation" lodging for servicemen. Many *kama'aina* still laugh about the underwear and socks drying in the windows of both hotels. Here at the Royal, a sailor looks over the semi-empty beach with only a few servicemen next door at the Outrigger Canoe Club. The barbed-wire barriers remained in place until 1943, when a Japanese invasion of the island no longer seemed possible. *Baker-Van Dyke Collection*

Beautiful hula girls in red, white, and blue cellophane skirts entertained the troops. *Baker-Van Dyke Collection*

In 1944, President Franklin D. Roosevelt came to O'ahu to consult with General MacArthur and Admiral Nimitz. The result of that fateful meeting was Roosevelt's decision to allow MacArthur to invade the Philippines and free the Filipino people as he had promised, without bypassing them on the push toward Japan. *Baker-Van Dyke Collection*

As Hawai'i entered the war in 1941, the government forbade most photography. Over 250,000 members of the armed forces poured into the studios of Ray Jerome Baker to be photographed, sadly for the last time. *Baker-Van Dyke Collection*

In August 1945 the war in the Pacific came to an end, and people went wild. Every street in Honolulu, from downtown to Waikiki, filled with celebrating sailors, soldiers, and civilians. *Hawai'i State Archives*

$\mathscr{A}$FTER THE WAR

Peace, calm, and happiness settled back to Waikiki after the war's end. Tourists and islanders returned to Kuhio Beach in the area of the old Waikiki Tavern. 1950. *Baker-Van Dyke Collection*

After VJ Day, the Royal Hawaiian Hotel needed two years to clean its carpets, remodel its exterior, and rebuild its dining room. Visitors did return, but slowly. Pan American World Airways started daily service from California in 1946 in new planes that took only 12 hours for the flight, down from the pre-war 16-hour trip. A one-way ticket cost about $100.

Many business leaders lamented that Waikiki had been killed off as a tourist destination due to the "jungle" atmosphere of bustling commercialism begun during the forties. "Is Waikiki Dead?" one newspaper editorial lamented in the early fifties. While tourism had never been higher than 30,000 visitors in the pre-war years, the prospect of postwar tourism continued to languish.

"Hawaii Calls," which had broadcast throughout the war, was the nation's most popular regular radio show in 1948, according to *Variety*. Spreading the word of Hawai'i as a visitor destination was boosted that year when businesses and the Territory raised $500,000 to promote tourism. Two years later, Waikiki was hosting 45,000 annual visitors, nearly double the number in the peak years before the war.

The International Market Place which opened in 1957, promised a new awakening of tourism in Waikiki. Its historic old central banyan tree, once on the estate of King William Lunalilo, graced the arts and crafts shops that offered travelers a taste of Polynesia and Asia. Original plans for the Market Place called for the construction of several "theme villages" where handicrafts from around the Pacific and Asia would be hand-made and sold.

"Anything can happen in Waikiki," remarked innovative hotel developer Roy Kelley in 1955 at the opening of his first ocean-front hotel, the 10-story 350-room Reef Hotel, next door to the Halekulani on Kalia Road. Already the former architect had built the successful Edgewater Hotel. It had Waikiki's first pool and first automatic elevator—*and it wasn't even on the beach!* With the Reef Hotel, Kelley single-handedly proved that Waikiki could be affordable and profitable in the growing "middle-income visitors" market.

The national media continued to help promote Hawai'i as a visitor destination. Arthur Godfrey, a frequent visitor to the Islands, used Hawai'i's ukulele as his trademark on both radio and television. James Jones' scorching novel *From Here to Eternity*, made into a great postwar movie in 1954, helped popularize Waikiki. Elvis Presley's hit film, *Blue Hawaii*, promoted the Islands with a new, younger generation. A common prize on America's daytime quiz shows became "a fabulous, all-expenses-paid trip for two to... HAWAI'I!!"

In 1955, visitor totals reached 105,000. During January, February, and March of that year, hotels were booked solid, and by the year's end 1,050 new rooms had been added to the inventory. But it was still not enough. In 1959, five airlines called an emergency meeting with Hawai'i's leading politicians and visitor industry executives to complain about the lack of hotel rooms. The airlines were having to turn away business. By 1960, another 2,000 new rooms were in the works. Roy Kelley had seven-year plans for 7,000 new rooms. "I just go out and build hotels," he said. "I don't talk about 'em."

A new era for Waikiki was initiated in 1959 when Hawai'i became the 50th State. Four-and-one-half-hour jet service from the mainland that same year marked the beginning of mass tourism; and the Boston-based Sheraton chain bought four of Waikiki's most prestigious hotels—the Royal Hawaiian, the Moana, the Surfrider, and the Princess Ka'iulani—for $118 million from Matson Navigation Company.

Among the most important steady visitors were the many World War II veterans who, two decades after the war, returned to the Islands of their youth with their families. By 1962, one million annual visitors were now coming to the Hawaiian Islands.

The arrival of jumbo jets in 1970 coincided perfectly with the arrival of jumbo hotels, most notably the Ala Moana Hotel with 1,300 rooms, the Hyatt Regency Waikiki with 1,200 rooms, and the huge but intensely efficient and profitable Sheraton Waikiki with 1,900 rooms. The Hilton Hawaiian Village on Waikiki's biggest parcel of land grew and grew until, by 1982, it was a 2,532-room high-rise city. The big jets delivered two million people in 1970, four million people in 1980, and 6.5 million in 1990. Waikiki was going dizzy in the upward swirl of hotels, people, and inevitable change.

"Diamond Head stands in a garland of waves." In this 1950 Ray Jerome Baker aerial view we see Kapi'olani Park and the Natatorium to the left, Le'ahi crater in the center, and on the horizon Koko Crater, Koko Head, and, to the far right, the island of Moloka'i. *Baker-Van Dyke Collection*

The Helumoa Coconut Grove on the beach fronting Kalakaua Avenue near Uluniu Street was eventually thinned to make space for new hostelries, taverns, and imported banyans. Trolley tracks, sunken into the paved asphalt, made the street a little bumpy for the new Fords and Chevys. Circa 1945. *Baker-Van Dyke Collection*

The white-shirted attendants at this Union service station on the corner of Kapahulu and Kalakau, filled your tank, washed your windows, and then gave you dinnerware as a gift for patronizing their establishment. Those were the good old days. Circa 1950. *Baker-Van Dyke Collection*

Beach services and surfboard rentals and Waikiki Tavern,
1950. *Baker-Van Dyke Collection*

Waikiki Tavern's "Merry-Go-Round bar," old Steiner home,
and Waikiki's beachfront bowling alley, 1950. *Baker-Van
Dyke Collection*

Waikiki Tavern on Kalakaua was a great bar and restaurant beloved by Hawai'i's young and old, 1950. *Baker-Van Dyke Collection*

The Waikiki Bowling Alley, 1950. When this building was demolished, the lost "wizard stones" were found in its foundation and moved to their present location on Kuhio Beach. *Baker-Van Dyke Collection*

The Hustace Villa, the site of which had been earmarked for development and would become the Surfrider addition to the Moana Hotel. *Baker-Van Dyke Collection*

Two shops at the front of the International Market Place were started in 1950 by Don Beach in conjunction with his famous Don the Beachcomber restaurant. By 1957 the Market Place was filled with many and varied shops and restaurants. Its banyan-bowered mall remains a must-see for first-time visitors to Waikiki. *Laurence Hata Collection, Bishop Museum*

Kalakaua Avenue crosswalk leading to Don the Beachcomber, 1957. *Laurence Hata Collection, Bishop Museum*

A young Hawaiian girl in one of the curbside lei stands. *Laurence Hata Collection, Bishop Museum*

The "Crossroads of the Pacific" sign at Kau Kau Korner, located on the site of the Hard Rock Cafe. Through the thirties and forties postcards of the sign outsold every other image of Waikiki except Diamond Head. *Baker-Van Dyke Collection*

On the sidewalk in front of the Outrigger Hotel, facing the Moana (the white building to the right) and Diamond Head at the end of the street. 1957. *Laurence Hata Collection, Bishop Museum*

WAIKIKI'S JOURNEY TOWARDS THE 21ST CENTURY

As Waikiki readies itself for the 21st century, many Island residents have attempted to peer into the future, to envision a Waikiki in 2020 A.D. Some seers portray a Waikiki of shaded sidewalks and broad promenades laced once again by 10,000 coconut trees, where high-density hotels are graced with huge open spaces and lush gardens. Some visionaries have even predicted off-shore, floating, man-made islands encapsulated in weather-controlled bubbles to accommodate the expanding population of O'ahu.

One aspect the visions share is that the special heritage and beauty of Waikiki must be integrated into any plan for the future. Many residents and repeat visitors have commented, "What has become of old Waikiki?" Has the commercial growth and vast expansion of visitor services diminished the aloha, beauty, and mystique which once charmed chiefs, commoners, and foreigners?

No longer can Waikiki claim to be as "quiet" as Robert Louis Stevenson observed it to be in 1893, but the rest of his encomium, the "lively scenery…pure air, clear sea water, good food, and heavenly sunsets hung out…over the pacific and the distant hills of Waianae"—these fundamental things still apply in the 1990s. The challenge for Waikiki 2020, will be to ensure, through continued effort, the enhancement of Hawaiian place names, to designate and properly interpret historic sites, and to expand the deep-seated Hawaiian values of aloha and *ho'okipa* or hospitality, so that visitors and residents of the future will know the beauty of this ancient place.

A visit to the sacred *pohaku* of Waikiki might be a starting point. Gathered together on Kuhio Beach, they symbolize that Waikiki remains a Hawaiian place with a rich heritage in spite of change. While much of the past has vanished, on those still nights when the glowing, full moon hangs above Diamond Head and the faint strains of a Hawaiian slack-key guitar waft in the air through the languishing palms, the magic of old Waikiki can still be felt. In the stories of yesteryear, spirits old and new are conjured up, keeping alive for future generations the mystique, romance, and enduring respect for beloved Waikiki.

"Mr. Morales" with a wooden Viking figure with famous signatures. Notice the different patterns in this composition—the thatching, the aloha shirt, the pants, the Viking's shining spear and helmet, the blotchy, rough carving, and Mexican fabric on the far right. 1959.
Laurence Hata Collection, Bishop Museum

A tourist couple going *makai* (toward the sea) on Lewers Road. They should trade shirts. *Laurence Hata Collection, Bishop Museum*

Kalakaua Avenue from the Moana Hotel, where the International Market Place, Liberty House, and Waikiki Theater are visible. 1968. *Laurence Hata Collection, Bishop Museum*

The beach at Waikiki in June 1950, with the Moana and Royal Hawaiian Hotels. *Baker-Van Dyke Collection*

The view from the Surfrider dining room. *Laurence Hata Collection, Bishop Museum*

Waikiki's streets often become a gathering place for *ho'olaulea* (celebrations) and parades as people from Hawai'i and around the world meet at this crossroads of the pacific. *Laurence Hata Collection, Bishop Museum*